SO

So

Steven Blyth

PETERLOO POETS

First published in 2001
by Peterloo Poets
The Old Chapel, Sand Lane, Calstock, Cornwall PL18 9QX, U.K.

**A catalogue record for this book is available
from the British Library**

ISBN   1-871471-98-2

Printed in Great Britain By
Antony Rowe Ltd, Chippenham, Wilts.

ACKNOWLEDGEMENTS

Acumen, BBC North West Radio, Magma, Nailing Colours Anthology (Commonword), Orbis, Other Poetry, Penniless Press, PN Review, Poetry Wales, Smiths Knoll, Staple, The Interpreter's House, The Rialto, Thumbscrew.

south west arts

To Robert and Lucy

Contents

Town Hall

It sat there like the head of a huge rivet
That held this town to the hills. For years, I worked inside.
My family, their friends and neighbours were impressed.
Not the security and good pension that did it,
More the building itself – columns, clock tower, ornate back gates.
And grandeur they'd only glimpsed paying the rent or rates –
Brass bannisters, bronze Greek gods, a stained glass coat of arms.
Dad told of his shop steward going to a meeting there,
Coming back wide-eyed as a conquistador
After seeing the cabinet of Mayoral silver.
A public place, they could have gone in, but didn't dare
As if scared off by the busts of Victorian fatsos,
Founders of the mills my grandma lost her hearing in.

I'd mention the miseries of such an old building –
Heating that rarely worked and when it did, the boiler's din;
Poor lighting, draughty windows, sometimes sludge from the taps.
I'd try to capture as well the dullness of the offices –
The shelves of files that looked like gills beneath mushrooms' caps,
Ones grown in damp patches left by the tears we were bored to.

The only perk of sorts was a basement that sprawled –
Great for a fag during a ten minute bunk.
Down there, rooms full of municipal junk;
In one, behind some rolls of worn red carpet,
A five foot statue of Eve, serpent at her feet.
Some joked it was the image of a councillor's wife,
Rumoured an ex-stripper who had an act with a snake.
She presided over talk about *our* Edens –
Fortnights in Spain, weekends in the lakes,
Or just Saturdays in the park with the kids and dog.
Upstairs, the bong of the clock like the anger of God.

The Candidate

Tonight, the lines on this sports centre's floor do not, for him,
Mark the territory of a flukey win

Like last week's five wheezing middle-managers
Who put two past a keeper who'd trialed for Spurs;

Instead, they're like the lines on astrologers' charts
That doom him to his handful of votes,

This Tory standing in a ward nicknamed New Stalingrad.
"He has a big family who turn out for him," is the usual gag

From those of us who run the count. In truth, he puzzles us –
Why stand year after year, as he does,

To take such a visible, public defeat?
The others who contest such safe seats

Can only bear it once or twice. Usually
They're flattered into it by their party's branch secretary

Or promised a sure win of a ward in next year's,
Its majority held out like a suitcase full of used tenners.

From the rostrum, he faces cheering red rosettes –
A gout of blood from his freshly guillotined neck.

The rest of the year, he's one of the Borough's success stories –
Owner of a small chain of shops. "Selling groceries,

Like Mrs. Thatcher's father," he's been known to say.
He's sometimes seen sorting out one of his window displays,

Tossing bruised fruit aside.

The Suitcase

Brown and battered, it seems as innocent as Paddington Bear's
Until you see what's scrawled on the side: *Exhibits – Sex Shop.*
It's tucked away in the Town Hall archive where I work, there
Since they closed one down in '74, its locks
Loose after twenty years of attempts to peek in.
Shake it and the sliding around of the few contents
Seems like the scurry of quarantined plague-rats.

The property of the then Deputy Leader, Councillor Hughes,
It was brought in to save office juniors from sin.
Churchman and war hero, the local Evening News
Claimed he pursued the closure in the same vigorous way
That he fought the Nazis in North Africa.
I imagine that case shrouded in steam at Manchester Victoria,
Him off for basic training, vowing to his fiancée
That he'll stay faithful if he's posted overseas.
The story behind his portrait fuels this image of them:
Painted to celebrate his OBE,
He wanted his wife on it too – "Behind all great men…"
The Council wouldn't agree, the compromise
Her favourite flowers – freesias – on the desk beside him. So
      romantic,
The story rivals the surrounding civic splendour.

Tells this to Alf, our neighbour, and he'll shake his head and grin.
He served in the same campaign as Hughes, remembers
Lectures in Cairo on spotting infection in your prick.
For men deprived for years of girlfriends and wives,
The whores were oases in vaster deserts than those they'd fought in.
"No one abstained. Most caught a dose, too. Like pissing glass!"

Just as they took the risk of catching the clap,
Phil and me take one on a bollocking from our boss:
We slide a steel ruler into the case; it cracks
Open like a delicious nut, but disappointment spills out –
Black and white mags lacking a single full-frontal
Of half-dressed, platform-shoed, winking women. Laughable,
Especially when I think of how its locks
Were always first to be tried with keys found astray.
Its own key left with Hughes when he retired, no doubt,
Perhaps now lies in some trinket box,
Is one of those things his widow can't bear to throw away.

Commuters

They're always on the eight o'clock to Oxford Road,
Wearing the same company ties.
Pete, Dave and Clive are the names I've overheard.

Pete and Dave pass charts between them
As excited as kids with notes
About secrets Clive isn't in on.

They talk about the latest sales figures
As if they are as thrilling as cup tie results,
Their team thrashing Clive's six nil.

Company papers peep from their brief cases –
Flags raised in the kingdom of the keen.
A sandwich box is all Clive carries.

Some might say Pete and Dave are slaves to work
But they look like freer men than Clive,
Who seems to wear a heavy suit under his pin-stripe.

Its weight makes him slouch in his seat,
Then slow to rise when we arrive,
Lag behind his two colleagues on the platform.

I sometimes think of Clive during my lunch break –
Though not a patch on evenings or weekends
Perhaps now his sleeves lighten a little at his desk.

Our junior spends his reading novels –
Always sword and sorcery or science fiction.
On the cover today, a man in chainmail and breastplate.

Take heart, Clive – he's slaying a dragon.

Memo to Colin

Back after my fortnight off,
I find your desk too tidy, mug near the window,
Oddly half full, a thin lid of mould on top.

Later, I'm told they thought you'd overslept again
On that dreadful morning last week.
Your heart seemed least likely to pack in,

Your days here so stress free – paper
Read from inside a file till nearly lunch,
Then tranny and ear-piece to catch the races.

Fed up by early afternoon,
I follow your example
And skive off to the basement strong-room.

You showed it me when I was a trainee.
Despite the ban, we stood there snug
In scarves of fag smoke, you telling me,

"First rule – never let them know you're slack.
Fake busyness or else they'll pile the work on."
You were expert at that –

Shuffling letters like a conjurer with cards
Whenever bosses were around.
Down here today the fluorescent tube has, aptly, gone.
No other trace of light gets in. A very real dark.

My eyes will not get used to it.

9 A.M.

Fluorescent lighting clatters on, sounds
Like footsteps – the day's dullness giving chase.
Beside the Xerox lies a mound
Of spilt toner – the ashes of the hours
I've spent in this place.

Sweet as splinters
Or nicks from some tool's blade,
Paper cuts are the only consolation
For hands too clumsy to catch trades
Tossed to them by my dad, granddad, uncle.

The first fax stammers from the machine
While my motives for sticking at this are still
Snug in their beds, on half term.
Tonight, I'll postpone fixing our leaky gutter.
Instead, I'll have some fun with them –
Turn up a CD or the radio;
From thin air, conjure a guitar,
Mime the solos.

Sweets

As odd as when a barman first called me *sir* and not *son*

To hear myself called *boss* for the first time.
It makes me wonder if Jill's offer of a chocolate lime

Is made out of pure generosity,

A friendly gesture to help the new man find his feet,
Or is, instead, an attempt to keep me sweet.

Not that she needs to bother:

I've worked for too long under bad bosses –
The rude, the cruel, the bullies, all labeled twats and tossers,

All becoming the butt of jokes about jackboots –

And vowed I'd never commit the same crimes.
So all week I'm relaxed about lunch times,

Say *Please, Thank you, You're very kind, If you don't mind...*

Give the work out fairly; and come the end of the week
It's my turn to bring in a bag of sweets.

They all take one; though later I spot some in the bin,

Realise they didn't dare refuse their earlier bosses.
"Please," I say. "You must treat me as one of you." I go back to my
        office,

Leave them nodding. I think *must* and *boss*. Hmm, sweet.

Worktown

In July 1998, Bolton Art Gallery held two exhibitions: Humphrey Spender's mass observation photographs of the town in the 1930's (which got the town dubbed Worktown) and Picasso's late etchings.

A bloke getting shampooed on the market is Spender's best:
PROF. H. FRYER – WORKING MAN'S HAIR SPECIALIST –

PREVENTS ALOPECIA, RINGWORM, SCRUFF, DANDRUFF.
It sums up how, back then, life's focal point was work.
Just a few shots of fun – Blackpool in the "52nd Week",
Their year's only full five days off;

Work ate up as much of their lives as it does wall space now.
The Picassos are from the South Bank Centre's touring show –

Clowns, matadors, Minotaurs, naked couples.
They have a look of being drawn for pure fun –
Doodles he might have done chatting idly on the phone.
The dashes of colour are like a party's spilt cocktails,

Each stroke like a streamer on the floor.
It's a party few attend for long. Spender gets more.

The two "comments" books capture things well.
Spender is a "joy", "great", "a sheer delight."
Among a little praise, Picasso's is peppered with "shites,"
As messily places as dollops of it tossed against the wall;

Plus there's the predictable, "My kid drew better when she was two."
Though I despise such Philistine views

I find myself thinking that Spender's is the greater art.
It's as if they're snaps from some cherished family albums,
One of which we carry in our breast pockets at all times –
A piece of steel over our hearts.

Love Poem

The sort the women hate,
Nickname something like X-ray specs,
Shudder if he comes near their desks.
The sort who calls the men *lads, chaps* or *mate,*
Grades typists by their fuckability.
Most places have one. Ours was Frank.

He told me he liked to study
Women asleep on his train into work.
He winked, said it was nice to think
That's how they looked in bed.
Once, one slept in the seat next to him, head
Lolling onto his shoulder. She dribbled.
He showed me the faint stain. He smiled
As if it was an epaulette
Denoting rank among his kind.

He had a point, I found,
Watching those on my train who slept,
Lips sometimes parted as if for a long deep kiss.
I liked it best when they snorted or snored;
It was as if a secret was being shared.

His wife, Jean, often phoned,
Reminding him to pick up the kids,
Get some cat food, a birthday card for her aunt…
I'd take a message if he wasn't around.
She'd call me "love." It felt like punishment.

The Sceptics

His earliest memory – watching the first men on the moon.
'69. That would make him just over one.

To think that those blurry pictures are still clear in his mind.

We won't have it. No chance. Surely he's mistaken,
Must have been older and watching some later Apollo mission.

But he insists. He gets back up

When we think our argument will keep him knocked down.
Just as he would have learning to walk back then,

Finding this new stuff underfoot so strange. Like Armstrong himself.

Art

"Draw that." He'd plonk down things like kettles and sheep skulls.
We'd struggle with the curves
While he turned his mind to a different kind –
Those freshly formed on certain fourth and fifth year girls.

He often told them if he won the pools
He'd chuck it in, open a chippy or pub.
Now, of course, I can see why – it made him seem closer,
Trapped in classrooms just like us.

He mentioned clubs he'd done gigs in.
That never failed to impress,
All places they'd been turned away from, despite thick make up.
Sometimes he strummed the guitar kept behind his desk;

Us boys and ugly girls reckoned he couldn't really play.
Still, he could draw; no doubting that one,
Proof in sketches he did of favourite girls.
We joked he wanted to do them with nothing on.

Years later, a story in the local news –
My school, a teacher, *Sex with pupils past and present.*
Unnamed at first, I guessed it was him.
Being right was like adding the last stroke to a portrait,

Sitting back smugly, awaiting admiration
As he used to after doing some busty brunette.
Then he'd dash round in the final minute,
Glance at the crap we'd drawn,

Say things like "nice" and "good."

Doing Time

So good to have met the devil and lived to tell –

The undivided attention of work friends and party guests,
Me appearing brave and interesting. Of all my stories, it's the best.

I went to school with a murderer.

The same class. In our fifth year when he did it. Nicknamed psycho
Because he chucked a chair through a classroom window.

He carried a knife. Showed me once. The one he used ...

No chance of us meeting again – you're still under lock and key.
Perhaps I should visit to thank you for this great story.

Little else to say. No polite chat as with other ex-school mates

About what we've been doing for the intervening years.
What could you say? Just, "Oh, this and that. Mainly pacing prison
     yards."

Telling your story so often and to so many for so long

And finding that getting a better one from my life is rather hard,
You could say I'm still pacing our old school yard.

Not much of a difference between us, then. Except that you want to
     be free.

Hard

I often see him here and there,
Think back to when, worried he'd wait at home time,
I'd alter assembly's Lord's Prayer
So it delivered me from him.

What I'd seen done to others
Ran through my head all day – rabbit punched; tripped,
Doc Martens landing on fingers;
Nose burst, teeth chipped.

Chicken pox saved my neck –
Some other first year had taken his fancy
By the time I was back.
Mum daubed Calamine all over me,

A warrior's woad, I'd pretend,
Standing at the window, on guard.
A huge pair festered on the back of my hand.
You can still see the scars –

Craters, the eyes
Of the man in the moon.
One is so faint these days
It seems they're winking, as if, I imagine,

Suggesting I should lighten up, forget this stuff,
We were kids, that's all.
But I remember my dad's bowie knife,
The day I slipped it into my satchel.

Lucky Stars

A friend during a fortnight holiday.
Pontins at Prestatyn, 1978.
At the junior pool table, he asked me to play,
Was much better but I won,

Him sinking the black. Unlucky.
It seemed he'd been so all his life,
Dad pushing off when he was a baby,
Mum dead when he was six,

Him now with a reluctant aunt.
Poor sod. She was a mean old cow –
Never let him wear jeans, just proper pants.
And worse that that, a tie.

It was just as well, reckoned mum –
The knot seemed all that held on his cousins' cast offs.
Dad said, "You should count your lucky stars, son,"
As he did when we passed kids in wheelchairs,

Or those he clipped my ear for calling "mong"
Still, he seemed happy enough –
Laughed at the magician's wilting wand,
Joined in the Kids' Club's games.

And while life had been cruel,
He could still enjoy boyish cruelties
Like squashing moths glued by the glare of the camp's loos;
Holding them, he could still feel terror as just a tickle.

Back home, though, I'd think of him as I lay in bed –
The horror of his aunt's cold bare spare room.
Watching the stars through the crack in my curtains
I'd remember dad's words, wonder if, instead,

He lay counting the dark bits in between.

The Café

We'd buy breakfast in there – cans of Coke
And Mars bars eaten on the bus to school.
Keith Stubbs (a lippy kid) asked the owner why
(Seeing as he didn't have to) he chose to wear a tie.
"Standards," he snapped. He had plenty of those –
Formica wiped within seconds of a spill,
Wet swirls from his mop often covering the floor,
Tea urn polished so well he could catch
Our tongues and two fingers behind his back.

Serving, his "Yes, sir" had a strong sibilance
As though he were piping people aboard
His tight ship, the only disturbance
The clatter of his wife in the back rooms.
We wondered why she stayed out of sight.
His hands were so big (like murderers' in films)
It made us think she might have bruises to hide.
The whoosh of his espresso machine
Soon started to sound like her scream.

One morning an early delivery of stock
Left him busy round the back. She served, shook
Dropping a plate, spilling sugar, someone's hot Vimto.
Clearly some illness. Parkinson's I'd now guess.
The truth was clear, too – he couldn't stand the mess
That's why she kept out of the way.

She had no change for my birthday fiver,
Said, "Pay me tomorrow. Don't tell him, though."
I never got the chance (things back to normal next day)
But wanted to, those coins feeling like pills – her cure.

Crimewatch

For Chris

Our school bully's on it. Not
As a bank job's blurry closed-circuit shot

But as a Detective Constable!

I shouldn't be too surprised – he joined the army
And we heard he'd gone into the MP.

He loved all that even then. A cadet,

He called himself "The Captain",
Made kids salute if they were smaller than him.

You'd been to the same primary school

And by secondary had taken enough of his crap.
You became like a last stand kamikaze Jap,

Whistling "Colonel bogey" when he passed,

Never wearing poppies, humming through Armistice's two minutes.
In '82 came one of your bravest moments –

"Argentina has a right to take the Falklands back."

*

I phone to say he's on TV.

We joke he'll have you nicked,
Beaten up in the cells till you admit

To every unsolved murder on the books.

Of course, I'd visit you in prison;
Would have to, you being Godfather to my son,

Each other's best man, holidays together, regular nights out.

And that's despite me standing by when he struck –
Five years of passing punches twice a week,

Pounced on at the gate after each term.

It makes me think it's me he'd arrest –
This friendship something I haven't earned, a kind of theft.

Young Men

The first naked women I ever saw in the flesh

Was in Ayckbourn's *Way Up Stream* at the local rep.
At the end a couple skinny dip

And did for real in this production.

A stir in the town. "Over 18 only" notes on the posters in shops.
At 16, a friend and me got in with comps

Given to us by an older friend who ushered there.

We wished the final scene on from our seats three rows from the front.
When it arrived, a standing ovation in our pants,

Then off for an underage pint and talk

About which bit of her we liked the best – tits, pussy, arse?
And whether the other actress

Would have been the better one to have seen – younger, slimmer

But, sadly, only bikini-clad in scene 4.
Finally, which of the two we'd like to fuck more.

Months later, the nude actress appeared in a washing powder ad

As a mum waving her son off to his first day at work,
Pleased with his "whiter than white" shirt

That had been smeared with mud the previous day.
Thinking of the way we'd talked, I felt dirty too.
But knew that was here to stay.

Science Fiction

It's life, Jim, but not as we know it
                    Dr. McCoy, Star Trek

Read now, it's funnier than the *Beano*

This early '60s sci-fi stories mag.
Less the evil three-armed Venusian Thrags

Or drawings of rockets that look like cigar tubes

And more the ads: one and six
Gets you *BLACKOE'S HANDY TRICKS,*

A pamphlet to make you "a real man;"

For tuppence more, a book to help those whose "character limps;"
For more still, there's *Dr. GOLDBRAIN'S PECTORAL PUMPS.*

All aimed at adolescent boys, the bulk readership.

I should know. At seventeen
I loved lightspeed, laser guns, time machines…

The ad's appeal, of course, is the chance to fast

Forward the day you stop feeling like a gangling goon,
Leave your bedroom's cocoon,

Where you've spent years reading about other worlds,

Able at last to grapple with this one. Adult to the core.
The day – as Blackoe puts it – that you are

"Capable and confident with cash, career, and kissing."

A day which – for them, for me, for most – never seems to have
     arrived,
As untrue as page four's prediction of men on mars by '85.

Life, Jim, but not as we want it.

A Common Interest

Most friends knew gold could kill a Cyberman,
That Davros invented the Daleks. A true fan,

Neil knew more. Things like what TARDIS stood for,
Impressing me, who got stuck half way: "Time and relative..er?"

A few years older, he remembered most of Pertwee
And even some of Troughton's stuff, like the famous Yeti.

More interesting by far than the lectures we met in –
Day release during my first short-lived job at seventeen.

Come weekend, I'd go to his flat and watch a video –
All six part of *Robots of Death* or *Sea Devils* – borrow

One of his Terry Nation paperback adaptations.
The friendship faded when I lost interest in science fiction.

Later, I heard Neil was gay from friends of a friend.
It left me wondering if he'd had more in mind

The time he suggested I stayed over. I felt disgust –
A straight male's gut reaction; felt like the scientist

At the end of the second part of *Ark in Space*
Watching his captain turn into leader of the alien race.

Still, it solved a puzzling event: the loos during lunch break,
Some bloke from our class punching me hard in the back,

My head hitting the wall, piss sprinkling my jeans. Scary.
He never said why. I dared not ask, just thought him crazy.

Now, I wonder if he knew about Neil, thought us a couple,
This my very own brush with queer bashing. Neil

Changed the subject when I told him – more series facts
Like how, being a Time Lord, The Doctor has two hearts.

The Wedding

To a genuine Hell's Angel this time. He's number four.
Riding pillion on his Harley, you roar
To the registry office; his chapter ride behind
Like some illegal exhaust emission.
You're wearing a black leather bikers' suit with tasseled sleeves,
Brag you found the right fit with the first you tried on –
"A good omen!" Apt also, to my mind,
For the way you always mould yourself to your husbands' lives,
Which are always odd. The first, a fairground man.
You claimed you loved that pokey caravan,
Learnt to run his dodgems, could soon leap from bumper
To bumper like one born to it. An actor next.
I'd get calls – "*King Lear* – what's the plot? Who's Brecht?"
It helped you laugh along with his green room banter.
You started wearing leg warmers and leotards, took up dance.

Today, headbanging replaces the bride and groom's waltz,
Metallica drowning your mum's sigh, "She thinks this stuff's awful."
Drowns too the words of sisters, aunts, great aunts,
Each like the punch that once got the best man done for assault –
Victim, loser, weak. These women are scornful
Of the way you never gain love on your terms,
Then still lose it – to Brighton rep's Desdemona,
To the daughter of the Big Wheel owner.
These women smile widely in your wedding albums
At whispered jokes about Elizabeth Taylor.
They wear anniversary jewellery, new hats and frocks;
Their husbands waited outside the fitting rooms
Like obedient dogs outside corner shops.

You jumped at the chance to join your third, a French sailor,
Were so sea sick you thought your cabin might end up your tomb,
Found only he spoke English (when he wasn't drunk)

And bugs from the hold's bananas in your bunk.
That – your briefest – was more than even you could bear.
Some good came of it – you no longer shrink
From lifting a huge spider from your bath or sink,
Touching something those women wouldn't dare.

Junk

Our rows' causes are always as lost as the moment we go
To sleep; we do that with our backs turned and wish
We were just a jailbreak's pillow fake,
The real one on the run from cutting remarks
That soon turn into blunt instruments –
A cup or plate or vase thrown in fury at the wall or floor.
This morning, I drop last night's shards into the bin.
Next, bacon under the grill. Enough for you as well,
Knowing you'll be down soon and we'll apologise,

Offered like the fragile champagne flutes that still survive,
Given to us by our honeymoon hotel.
Before that, the post arrives – news I could win
A car if I order a remote control garage door;
Offers of two credit cards with no fee and lower interest rates;
A travel brochure with free flight-times charts.
In the bin too, of course. It's good to wake
To something that, asking myself, "Do I really want this?"
I can say with certainty, "No."

Double Divan

When our radio alarm goes off this morning
They're playing, *You've been Talkin' in your Sleep*.
I reach out to retune it, get dance music, beat
As fast as our hearts in earlier days
When waking together was still a thrill.
Others mightn't have saved you from that song, might've let it play
As punishment – laying on the guilt
Like the pillow they might wish you smothered with.

A week since that club, you coming home at four,
Crashing into bed beside me, moaning his name, "John",
As innocently as a snore
Or your usual dreamy nonsense we've always laughed about.
In fact it felt almost funny finding out that way –
Like being in a sitcom or *Carry On*.
Is this why I find it so easy to forgive you?
Hard to know exactly. Am I good? Is it love?
Perhaps it's because I believe your claim
Of no sex, just a "snog" – a stupid lump of a word
Not worth the effort of holding on to.
Worse, is it because I suspect I'd do the same?

First thing next morning, I slammed the front door
(Confronted, you'd confessed). By ten, I was cold and bored,
The whole thing just like walking off a headache.
Home, I hugged you in the hall. You sobbed, said sorry.
You'd tidied up. To welcome me back, perhaps,
Or an attempt to please like a child in disgrace.
The bedroom was no longer strewn with socks and undies,
The lot shoved in respective drawers.
Peeping from yours, some white lace.

Broken Glasses

Half-serious, you claim it's a divine punishment,
Struck blind for a night spent

Staring at your work-friend Julie at her 21st –
Cleavage, little split in her mini-skirt…

Undressing for bed, you ask if
I still find you "physically attractive?"

Like most people our age, you've started to worry
That this bit is getting too fat, that bit too saggy.

Your frown shows you think I've lied when I answer, "Of course;"
For that, too, I deserve this biblical-style curse.

It seems almost plausible for a moment – snapped
Across the bridge while they were being wiped,

No pressure to break what have survived sitting-ons and falls.
Still, I'll have none of it. A simple mishap,
Me never one for a belief in God. Nor angels.

Man and Boy

First, two holes hacked in the lawn he knows I love.
They stared up when the curtains were opened
Like this eight year old's eyes (pure hate)
When I pass his garden. The gate's closed –

No more pavement ambushes, his *bang! bang!*
And my staggering, hammy *You got me.*
He holds the toy gun tighter, stays silent,
Thinks *Pretending's no longer enough for you.*

His mum says he's off most men these days,
Even granddad and his favourite uncle.
You can't blame him. Three months since the night
His dad walked out. Now in Cardiff with his aunt.

Not a visit or a phone call since then.
Men! Shits! As one of this treacherous lot
I deserve all I'm getting. Right now
He'll be piling leaves on my path, a few

Surprises inside – bricks and turds from his dog;
Or smearing mud on my car or lopping off
The heads of my daffs (next no doubt my cats).
Sometimes I notice his bedroom light on

In the early hours as I feed our baby girl.
Planning tomorrow's assault? More likely
A vigil for the postman. A lonely boy
Wishing for letters, postcards. *Please.* Unlikely.

Perhaps I should toss stones at the glass – come down! –
Go adventuring and form a blood brother bond.
But how to make sure the window won't break
When throwing with these arms – big, strong, grown up.

"As Long As There's Nothing Wrong With It"

It's most people's concluding phrase
After daft chats about which sex we'd like
Or jokey hopes it won't turn out like uncle Dave.
And though the signs and tests are fine,

Tonight's TV still leaves me worried – 2am;
An autistic kid digs and yells in a neighbour's garden,
His parents trying to coax him in;
They say this is an easy night for them.

It triggers thoughts of my friend's sister, Claire –
Her crumpled words, her fits,
The way she'd rock in that little wheelchair,
Flap like a landed fish when out of it;

It's as though she lived as briefly, reaching just four.
I try to think of happy moments,
Like the day we built her a snowman,
Our joy at its stumpy existence beyond the thaw.

Poem

(For my new born son, Robert)

There'll be no poem about you.
One about things like the day you were born,
Your christening and first birthday, no doubt,
In which, of course, you'll play a big part,
But there'll be nothing solely about you.
My poems are little stories,
Not the sort that reflect on single things –
Not even the orange I had with my lunch
Never mind a loved one.
I can't pluck you from narrative's river bed,
Hold you up to the light and see pure you.
I've had a bash. No luck. Sorry.
My eyes just don't work that way.

They say that for these first few weeks
Your eyes can see angels and ghosts.
I've read that soon they'll change from baby blue;
Probably to my side's plain brown.
This gives me hope you'll understand one day.
Not that I ask forgiveness.
I know it isn't always needed.
Waking to your cry has taught me this.

3 A.M. Feed

Soon we abandoned our "turns". I volunteered
Finding that, alone, the world hushed, I could almost hear

It whispered – "This is your son."

In the crook of my arm, a perfect fit,
You were those words given weight.

Your fish mobiles made it seem we sat on the sea bed,

Your bottle a little oxygen tank,
Your gentle sucking like a tick, tick, tick

Timing how long before we had to go up,

Face currents that tugged us apart - the fuss
Of want-to-hold relatives and, worse, the office

That kept me from your first step, first clear word.

Those moments were in the presence of grandparents and mum,
Remembered in detail – *Ten past one,*

Blur on the radio; he went from the armchair

To the coffee table. Still, for me,
Those feeds have equal clarity,

Last week coming so strongly to mind –

Caught T-shirted in a summer storm,
My forearm felt drops as large and warm

As the one I'd splash there to test the temperature.

That white drop would sometimes dribble
Down to my palm – a pearl.

So

A kid's funeral on the news. Cameras pan
Along rows of school friends' flowers and cards.
"We will always love you so very much," one reads.
"So" has been squeezed in. Neater. Different pen.

We guess it's been done by a dad or mum.
"So" – such a soft, small, sibilant word,
Like the sound of our baby's breaths when whispered.
His cot by our bed, we strain to hear them,

Thinking of when they'll blow out birthday candles,
Fill bubbles, or push a paper boat.
We leap up at any spates of strange gurgles.
One of us holds him till the breaths regulate.

Sometimes, then, we hear a question posed:
There's love and strength in your arms – So? So? So?

Mother's Day

That it only took one to undo a bra strap
Is about all these hands once bragged. Now they have the knack

Of nappy changes, bath time's slipperiness.
Watching me, people are impressed.

"New man", you sneer, complain that everyone expects you
To have these skills. "They think for women it's innate." True,

Though I know what fuels such feelings – he was first held by me;
The caesarean meant you were too sore and drowsy.

Today, I give you a card and a box of chocs.
My *To mum from Robert, love you lots,*

Is in my usual scrawl, the box badly wrapped,
As if to show there are still things at which I'm crap.

The Christening

Distressed, your heart-rate dropped, then soared,
The monitor's strange thrup, thrup, thrup
Like our cats scratching on the nursery door.
In the end, an emergency caesarean.

As I put on the greens, I whispered
Please God, please God, please God. Meant it.
Scared in the past I have, of course, hoped
But have never been one for *that* kind of plea –

Not even on that flight to Hong Kong
In storms so bad the crew were just as terrified.
Seven pounds one, the midwife told us. Wrong –
You were (still are) all heaven's weight

Under which my atheism buckles.
When you smile at blank walls and ceilings
I can almost believe it's at the angels
They say all babies see.

And so I don't feel such a hypocrite doing this.
Find it easy to put my trust in Christ,
To speak up when I make each promise,
To hear you cry at the water's cold touch.

Small Items of Power

Wallet, credit cards, TV remote control,
Wristwatch, mobile phone… He wants to hold them all,

Understands the importance they have in our lives.
And him only eighteen months old. Everyone nods and smiles,

Says it was much the same with their kids.
One of my mum's favourite stories

Is about me grabbing her purse, opening it,
Coins rolling all over the supermarket

Like drops of spilt mercury.
This morning, he drags my car alarm fob and key

From the dressing table. He dances and jangles them
Like a witch doctor with a magical charm.

I start with, "Please. Daddy's." Soon it's "Do as your told!"
I end up having to pull them from him.
He then shows me his growing grasp of this field –

Refuses me a goodbye kiss.

Phone Call

It's my wife. I say, "Can I help at all?"
Making it seem like any other business call;

My boss hates personal ones, is at a nearby desk.

She tells me our year old son's been slapped across the face.
Someone's toddler. Unprovoked. In the post office.

"What did you do?" Angry, I stay as cool as I can

So my boss will think it's just some overpaid account.
She told the toddler's mum she was a bad parent,

Had a nasty child; shamed her in front of the queue.

Her raised voice made the toddler shake and whimper.
I smile, imagine her like a warrior

Turning her spear in her opponent's guts.

Kids being kids, this won't be the last time it'll happen;
I promise myself that if I'm there, I too will step in,

Won't give my dad's advice to me: "Hit them back."

He showed me how to punch for a knock out:
"Pretend they're three feet further away; aim through, not at."

I never did, knew he hadn't too.

"Things OK?" My boss asks when I put down the phone.
I make for the gents, saying things are fine.

Alone in there, I kick the door, let my rage show.

Green disinfectant colours the water down the loos.
We had the same stuff at school.

I remember its taste, a fifth form hand on the back of my head.

Gyp

A Boxing Day party at our house.
A fuss when I find two hard stumps in our son's mouth.

"All I want for Christmas is my two front teeth," mum sings.
My granddad pulls his out, gives one of his gurney grins.

He laughs at both, but what best holds his attention
Is the sharp rattle of my bottled extraction,

As if he hears in it all my paternal side's teeth speak
About the bad luck that sticks in them like strands of tough meat.

For us, ice cream is like chewing a knife,
Jaws swell to look like Desperate Dan's, gum disease is rife.

My cousin, Paul, says to him, "Welcome to the family curse,"
Nudges me, whispers the first line of *This be the Verse*.

With luck, his will take after my mum's or wife's side.
If not, his only hope is that he'll be skipped.

It happens. Take my dad's cousin, Marge – a perfect set.
Mind you, that smile was her ruin claims aunty Bet:

Four marriages, her adulterous in them all.
A life of midnight flits and notes in the hall.

She had two children with the first.
He moved abroad with them. She seems unhurt,

Though it's said it saw off her dad before his time.
She's here today, parading a possible number five,

Passing round those chocolates of her sister's.
Perhaps we should hate her for being callous, fickle, sly...
Instead, we say "Thanks," go for the soft-centres.

Second Place

Just as we've decided to stop
Now we have her, Lucy, our second child,
    I feel I should also stop
Writing this "baby stuff." Our first child

    Meant that I did to death new life;
New subjects are what's needed in my poems,
    What count in this literary life.
So when I hear the patter of her poems

    I'll leave them at a door or – more
Effective – out for the wolves' teeth and paws,
    Concern myself with art worth more
Because it's unmarked by grubby little paws

    And gleams in the critic's light
Like antiques afforded by saving on
    The household bills – water and light.
But, mostly, it's warmth that I'll have scrimped on.

No. 3

5.30 am. Hard to sleep in this July heat.

Even harder with the worries we have
About two nights ago – making love

Followed by you forgetting your pill.

A habit you've fallen out of
After the pregnancy with our second. Two's tough enough

And thoughts of a third terrify us,

Fear so strong it beats my fear of hospitals –
I've agreed to let their scalpels near my balls!

We hear the gate creak, footsteps up and down the path,

As if our unborn third has tried
To glimpse the life it'll be denied

Before traipsing away sadly. I'm sad too, then –

We've abandoned it. Haven't enough love left. Our "No!"
Ordering it into some corner of a cruel limbo.

Later, there's milk bottles on the doorstep

Like sentries guarding against such irrational thought.
Of course, of course – it was the milkman's feet.

How dumb of me. What's never been

Can't shed tears over not being, can't feel rejected.
At the open door, I soak up the sun.
Another glorious day ahead.

I take in the milk before it sours.

November the Sixth

The smell of smoke in my clothes is like something nasty that's spread,
Fireworks in the garden seem like blackened crops;
The bonfire's dry ashes – as grey as the morning's cloud –
Are like the first fragments of a sky starting to collapse.

Today, mum gets her biopsy and blood results.
Last night she insisted we do things by the book –
Fireworks in a tin, spent sparklers dunked in buckets.
And she made sure we stood well, well back,

As it seems she has from us lately,
The needle's bruise on her arm all that gave things away.
No clue in what she said or did, dad sworn to secrecy.
"I didn't want you to worry. I'll be okay."

That said, I can't believe she'll soon walk to the hospital
Without seeing the burnt world as bleakly as I do.
Though when I phone to wish her well,
She still won't let fear through,

Changes the subject to our son, her first grandchild,
The rockets she pointed out to him, his "Ahs!" and "Ooos!"
It made being out in the bitterly cold night worthwhile.

Decorating the Living Room

To shift the sanding's dust and smell of drying gloss,
The door's half open. Dad offers a tentative, "Hi",
Enters as nervously as the neighbours' cat,
Daren't give advice on my DIY,

Knowing it will be cast aside like the badger hair brushes
He gave me when I set up my first home.
"They'll last a lifetime if you treat them well."
Forgotten for days, they dried solid. Beyond hope.

He watches in horror, as if my pasting table is the rack,
Me tightening it mercilessly as I do two more sheets
In ways he wouldn't dream of, his own matched-up
Perfectly, not one bubble or crease.

Unable to bear anymore, he makes some coffee.
I stop, steer clear of decorating as we finally chat,
Stick to the day's headlines – how the government
Wants Freemasons to name their membership. "Masons! Prats!"

Says dad. "Don and Phil once approached me to join.
Daft and sinister. I told them to stuff it."
I feel proud he turned down what I hate – that exclusivity
That seems designed to make others feel like shit;

Proud he had the conviction to let pass
What could have peppered his life with perks.
Not that I wasn't proud before – now a dad myself
I know that keeping it all together is damn hard work.

But that pride feels commonplace; this kind is like that felt
When someone close scores the winning goal or run.

He's come first in *Living Up To The Ideals Of Your Son.*
Olympic champ in it; world record breaker.

He toys with my plumb line's weight as if it's his medal.

The Soprano

Dashing out before five for rehearsals
You'd rustle up that awful stew;
I'd moan, scowl ballooned in the back of my spoon.
Worse, I had to watch those musicals,

Bored, arse aching on wooden church hall chairs.
Still, for a lad my age there were consolations –
Girls in leotards in the chorus lines;
Best when they were the Red Shadow's belly dancers.

Plus the giggle of hearing dad mutter "poofda"
When you had to kiss the leading bloke –
Insult, of course, but you said it was also part hope.
And funnier still was my grandma

Who didn't know the meaning of mutter.
Though you had "a lovely voice", she'd loudly criticise
The naff costumes, duff notes, baritone's glass eye.
In fact, everything that proved it amateur.

Once, hunting for Christmas presents in your wardrobes,
I found a reel of tape marked "Radio Shows",
Programmes with your name nearly top of the bill, photos
Of you singing in snazzy clubs.

From downstairs came the flat slap of your knife.

Dad's Early Retirement

He talks excitedly, as if these stories about the depot
Are jackpots from the pub's fruit machine. Then, "I miss it, you know,"

As if it's dawned on him that they're really a handful of coppers.
It explains his invitation out – I'm a useful pair of ears,

Mum bored by it, him only meeting ex-work mates once a month.
I tell him the last time we drank together was on my 18th

Which sets him off about when he was that age – an apprentice.
Funny, the way he still says "Mr" when he mentions an early boss –

Mr. Moston, Mr. Bracegirdle, Mr. Sumner. A small point
But it's like some archeological fragment

From which you can prove the power of an ancient empire.
When the pool table's free, I butt in, "Come on. I'll play you for a
      beer."

I stroke my cue like Nero with his bow.

Lance Corporal Blyth

Sunday school Christmas party, 1947.
My dad was scared of Santa,
Wouldn't go up for his present.

Funny thing is, it was his dad.
Not that he knew, of course;
Understandable, perhaps, if he had,

My granddad being a tyrant, it seems –
Too strict, too quick to raise his hand.
The army, that's what my dad now blames –

Posted to North Africa for the war,
My granddad didn't see his son
'Till he was four;

After years of discipline and tidy kit,
He was unable to cope
With the kerfuffle of a kid.

Granddad once showed me snaps
Of those desert rat days –
Daft baggy shorts, a silly hat,

Big clownish boots.
I giggled at him;
He giggled too.

Gob

For Tony Harrison
"Nice Poems. Don't care for the accent much."

A small lump under my tongue.
That comment made it seem apt –
A wart for an ugly accent.
My wife overheard it at my reading, kept

It to herself as if it was news
Confirming my worries about the Big C.
In truth, those words were no great shock –
Among voices closer to R.P.

(The sort my family and neighbours would claim
"Sound posh to the likes of us")
The clunk of my broad Bolton vowels
And my sibilants' buzz

Seem like the sound of some faulty machine.
I've often tried to keep it hidden,
Clinging to my Hs as if they were shields –
Teaching, job interviews, phoning London...

In the end, the lump was nothing –
A stone formed over the years in a saliva duct.
The clue to the diagnosis came when I ate –
One side of my neck swelling up.

Gone now, I can spit with the best of them.

Funny Business

THOMPSON'S reads the sign over the window.
In smaller letters, *Dancewear, Novelties, Fancy Dress.*
There a good fifteen years or so,
It's known as simply the joke shop.

Inside, the owner's on the verge of a sale –
He strokes the leather upper like a pet;
"That's a genuine Cuban heel."
The customers comment on his ballroom trophies.

"I was taught by Mrs. Moss of Blakely."
They've heard of her, seem impressed.
"Partnered in class by her husband, Ernie.
That's when he had both arms, of course."

Rooting through the racks of fancy dress, I grin,
Imagining Ernie's arm torn clean off
In some complex Latin spin.
Next, he gives the facts – accident in a paper mill,

Other arm left leaning on a walking stick.
His fault, they said. No chance of comp.
Now the owner seems heroic –
To think of life's sadness and horror,

Him still able to spend his time selling plastic boobs,
Silly String, fuzzy orange wigs;
And dry cleaning costumes like the clown's I choose.
(It's for a friend's birthday party. Her idea of fun.)

Taking it back a few days later,
I catch his daughter trying on dance shoes,
Tilting her foot to the mirror.
She kicks them off, moves to the till.

Her walk shows some problem with her hips.
I imagine her steps in the shoes –
Just slow, slow. Slow, slow. No quicks.
I spot him pricing-up stock in the back –

Stink bombs, powders to make you fart or itch.

Numbers Up

You gasp clearing your Great Uncle's house.
A changed will? Letters from an affair?
Instead, simple work days souvenirs –
Apprentice 90, loom 9, 9th floor.
You explain: "This house is number nine.
He was born on September the ninth.
Named Alexander – nine letters there.
His clapped out car's reg, J999."
It's as if he hoarded that number,
Hoards being his generation's thing.
When my Grandma died, her spare room held
Fourteen unopened tins of biscuits,
Eighteen loo rolls, thirty-one light bulbs,
Twenty tins of beans… Like King Tut's tomb.
Dad said it was because of the war –
"She still worried about shortages."
Was his nine-heap to prove the power
Of things you'd have to have faith in then?
Things like coincidence, luck and fluke.
A bullet bouncing off your fag case
As you charged across the D-day beach;
That bomb hitting the street's empty house
Or dangling from the rafters, a dud,
As harmless as a Christmas bauble.
News footage through NATO's cross-haired lens –
The nearest our generation gets.
Our remotes are boxes of numbers.
We can pick as many as we want.
Like chocolates. Enough to make us sick.

Least

My grandma died when she was ninety-one.
Terry at work made an attempt at consolation –

"At least she had a good innings.
I'd sign a contract for that." I started imagining

A dotted line that guaranteed
Nothing that smacked of Faustian greed

But instead a list of life's grateful "at leasts",
Things like *having your health*, a marriage that lasts,

Kids who *do well* at school, enough money to *get by*,
To know for certain that when you failed you gave it your best try…

Lucifer, Mephistopheles, Beelzeboul & Co, Solicitors.
"Sign here." You sweat in one of their red leather chairs,

Nervously eyeing the paperweight – a pickled soul.
Don't worry. When – nine years from your century – you're bowled

It'll be as if you slipped in the clause "last laugh."
You'll leave them empty-handed. What else after that kind of life?

Crap

My great aunt Elsie and great uncle Arthur
Had a fortnight's leave romance, were married months later.
Outside the church, they look happy, relaxed,
Smiles as magical as early colour,
So unlike most other 'forties photos –
Everyone stern and stiffly posed
As if they've got broom handles up their backs.

In 'forty-five their dream of a tripe shop opened.
Hard to imagine days of enough demand.
Comically Northern, it would be funny
If it wasn't for him upstairs, groaning to his end
From some terrible kidney disorder.
The family rumour is he caught it from water
Poisoned by the Germans in Normandy.

She tried to keep things going when he'd gone,
Blamed the tripe when severe colitis came on.
The friend she left in charge fiddled the books
During her weeks of hospitalization.
Better but broke, she had to sell the place,
Went back to the family terrace
To help her mum drag round her sack of minor aches.

She's never remarried, despite keeping her looks
Well into her seventies, valentine
To several blazered blokes.
And she still suffers from the runs now and then,
Claims it helps if she avoids red meat,
Rich sauces, anything too sweet.

Holiday of A Lifetime

My wet trainers squeak on the home's tiled corridor.
Even that seems too loud for 2am;
Grandma once would've said, "Means you haven't paid for them."
Friday. Now, eight hours behind us,
Mum and dad will have just arrived in Vegas,
Two-thirds through their three week west coast tour,
All thanks to dad's retirement lump sum.
Of course, we'll fix the funeral for when they're home,
But my sister, me and our Aunty May
Agree it's unfair to spoil it with this news; what's more
We can't bear to break it to mum so far away.

In turn we hold grandma's hand, kiss her. Still warm.
They serve us tea in the TV room.
Later, we put away the hankies, unfurl
Instead the funny stories granddad used to tell.
Comic book stuff, some about *their* holidays:
Pontin's mainly – he won the knobbly knees three years in a row;
In the ballroom dancing contest she broke his toe.
Once, they camped, tent sliding away in the mud,
Blown down when, chewed by a goat, their guy ropes snapped.
The strangest tale's about a swarm of flies in Fleetwood.
"Bloody Biblical, it was," Granddad said.
Her Alzheimer's started soon after that,
As if she'd swallowed some and they buzzed in her head,
Banged off her mind's windows.

Another pot of tea, then we go,
Passing a box holding flash cards, plastic shapes, a beach ball.
Therapy to try and keep other sufferers sharp.
On the wall, a kids' calendar and weather chart:
Today is Thursday. It is dull.

A Few Words

This small blank card seems like one of my answer sheets
In those remedial class tests –
I'd get so stuck I couldn't even guess.
When mum and dad returned from their tour of the states

It felt similar – my hesitation,
Unsure of what to say,
My sister's sudden tears giving it away
Just like when some smarter kid butted in.

The card's to go with a floral GRANNY;
A compromise after squabbles over GRANDMA or GRAN,
Price of the letters now neatly split between six grandchildren.
I feel as though I've bought the G –

First letter because I was her favourite
And also standing for "graduate",
The family's only one – the boy who went from thick to swot,
Bamboozling them with fancy words. Clever dick.

Still stumped, I ask my wife for a suggestion.
She gives me a stock phrase about being "greatly missed."
Again it's as if I'm sitting in a test,
This time one of those I cribbed in.

Once, a teacher hauled me out for it,
Called me a cheat.

Late

Part of their work was to rescue people who were put away for life not because they were dangerous to society, but only because they were disturbed and difficult... It was the law at the time that if a certified person could live undetected in normal society for six weeks, they were automatically decertified.

The Independent, 30th November 1998

He was late home from work that night. Too late
To make it another "cry for help", another scar on the wrist.
And I found out too late. At seventeen,
A drunken slip up by one of his mates.
"My Uncle Ken's *first* wife? What do you mean?"
Too late meant I was angry – how dare he insist
(As I was told he had) that us kids shouldn't know;
He'd even confiscated and hidden photos.

I remembered his christening gift to me. A wooden train. Favourite toy
Right up till I was five or six. He'd smile: "I bought well."
Just him? For my first six months her life overlapped.
Even that gentle boast came to seem part of his ploy,
Made that train seem to have been cheap splintering crap,
Me choking forever on a snapped-off wheel.
Perhaps I had no right – I hadn't suffered his grief –
But when he was around that anger rose as if

I was charging up stairs to free her from his spare room. The wanker!
Things changed when – in on the secret now –
I picked up the family view of her – maligned
As a mad witch, the selfish bitch who nearly took him with her.
I get it, Ken – rather no memory of her than one ruined.
Don't worry. In that spare room, I find an open window.
Too late. Just the faint trace of feet on your muddy lawn.
A mug of coffee on the sill. Still warm.

Hit and Run

She'd spend weekends with her big navvyish dad
Who, since it happened, has seemed like the elm
Earlier joyriders snapped.

Most trees round here have lost bark to their bumpers.
When I heard the thud that evening,
I thought they'd hit another.

I ran out, saw blood blooming on her Sunday dress,
Her tread-marked doll, her dropped-egg of a head,
Ran back to call the ambulance.

They asked if it was left at Bradford Road,
Then left again and second right?
The voice was calm, casual as those

That stop to ask for the Tescos lying nearby.
Last week, I saw him pointing the way,
Then return their kids' giddy wave, his arm raised high,

As if reaching to pick fruit.

Outer Space

Our neighbours' curtains were closed for two months,
Their three-legged cat being let in and out
The only sign of life. Weirdos. Psychopaths?

Paul down the street, 12 year old UFO fanatic,
Reckoned it was to block out the sun
As they recreated the conditions on their home planet

On which, of course, all cats have three legs.
He has every X Files episode taped,
Books with those pictures of frisbeed saucepan lids,

Believes the Nazcan lines are landing strips,
That Stonehenge was an intergalactic Heathrow,
That some tomb paintings show space ships.

His mum says he's a bad mixer
To explain his walks during school hours,
As dreamily distant as his Andromedan Nebula.

I saw him one afternoon, holding his coat open wide
As he leant into that day's gale,
Going so far he stumbled forward,

Embracing gravity.

Superstitions

Out for the night, we leave the hall light on –
Safer to suggest someone's in. Today, the bulb's gone.

The up-lighter shade cups some dead spiders.
I swirl out their webs like candy-floss with my screwdriver.

It's as if they were spun to blot out the bulb's light,
Them wanting us back in the days of oil lamps, candles, flint,

Days when, superstitions stronger, they had more influence –
It meant money if one fell on your face,

Good luck if one clung to your clothing,
One worn live in a bag cured most things.

Legs folded in, each looks like an apple pip,
As if it is their dying hope

That I'll count them, chanting *tinker, tailor, soldier, sailor...*
Instead, I drop them onto a page from the local paper,

Note its stories of poormen, beggermen, thieves.

Postcards

In October 1999 police arrested peaceful protestors during the week of the Chinese president Jiang Zemin's state visit to the UK.

I always sent one to my great aunt.
Even on day trips. She didn't care.
She liked them. And now I've inherited the box.
The most impressive is from China – aerial shots
Of the Forbidden City and Tiananmen Square.
The ballpoint's faint, my hand hesitant

As guilt tugged at it – the wonder
Of the Great Wall… "I wouldn't have missed
The Terracotta Army for the world. Magnificent…"
But all the time feeling every Yuan I spent
Went into the palm of the iron fist,
Was clenched to make its punch harder.

Most of the others are from British resorts
Like Skeggy, Morcambe. Fairgrounds and donkeys,
The kids beating me at soccer on the sands.
Good times. And all in a firmer hand –
No guilt about fun in a free country.
And look at this, the sort

I sent when my teens started to dawn –
A cartoon Queen bare-arsed on the beach, towel
Slipping as she tries to get changed.
On the back I mention that it rained.
Being Britain, that's on most of these. Often, just showers,
But always enough to leave me feeling let down.

Excuses

Men with unusually long ring fingers are more likely than most to feel depressed… The effect of the male hormone testosterone on the developing foetus was thought to be responsible. Testosterone affects the development of fingers and thumbs

The Independent

Page fourteen's feature
Is more like, for him,
The agony aunt –
It's not your fault, dear.
You're prone to these moods.
Loved ones must put up.
It means its knuckle
Need never again
Go nervously white
Helping clutch flowers,
An apology
For another night
Punching walls, doors, her.
Home, he lies his hand
Flat on the table,
Harmless. He explains
How it pulls his strings.
He raises it. Stiff,
Quivering slightly,
It looks like his cock
Before one of their
Kiss and make up fucks,
An act that appals
And puzzles her friends.
For years they've offered
Spare beds and sofas –
"As long as you need."
They are strong fingers.
She knows that too well.

But can't help feeling
Some pity and care
For this one, weakest.

The Climb

The first shot of you is well framed, has little sway,
Despite so much bare flesh. Preserved. Ghostly blue.
At this point, you're just another body on their search.
So many. Even now, one in six die up here.
For hours it's been, "No. That glove's too modern." Sighs.
Your shirt's name tag is what makes the camcorder quiv-
Er. An avalanche of excitement: *George Mallory.*
"Jesus! It's him! We've done it! Oh Jesus Christ!"
And you are a kind of Christ to these men,
Disciples who want to spread the word
That you got to the summit first, their miracle-proof
The camera with the negative showing you there.
No luck. But the facts of your fall – how, where –
Are enough for these experts' faith: "We now know his route,
Are sure he made it." Though there's one insight they're spared:
How it felt knowing – companion dead, your legs broken –
That it was a foothold in history you'd lost,
Certain some future climber would take the glory,
You left dangling on the platitude "brave."
Did you manage to slip away satisfied
Simply because you'd done it; no need for the cheers?
That's a peak which is even harder to reach.
But I like to think you made it there, too,
And from it could see as far as this day.